Choosing Christ

31 DEVOTIONS FOR HURTING HEARTS

Evelyn Collins

ISBN 978-1-63814-490-8 (Paperback)
ISBN 978-1-63814-491-5 (Digital)

Copyright © 2021 Evelyn Collins
All rights reserved
First Edition

Covenant Books, Inc.
11661 Hwy 707
Murrells Inlet, SC 29576
www.covenantbooks.com

To my dear friend Kathi,

She urged me to step out in faith
and was the instrument God used to ignite
and fulfill his divine purpose for my life.
We will meet again in heaven.
Forever in my heart.

Evelyn

CONTENTS

INTRODUCTION

You hold in your hand the result of many hours and years of my relationship with God. Since I was young, I poured out my heartfelt thoughts, hopes, dreams, and hurt to God in a journal way before it was popular.

Over the years, I yearned to hear his voice, and he answered me in a very personal way. He sometimes woke me up at night, and I scribbled his messages onto paper. His messages kept me focused on him, and I overcame doubt and fear.

During this Pandemic, I felt his prompting to help others who were confused, suffering, and had lost all hope. It is for him and his love for you that you hold this book in your hand.

My prayer for you is from the Word of God.

> The Lord bless you and keep you; the Lord make His face to shine upon you and be gracious to you, the Lord lift His countenance upon you and give you peace. (Numbers 6:24–26)

ACKNOWLEDGMENTS

Thank you, Lord, for the journey. I fall more in love and dependent upon you each phase of writing this book. I am so thankful for your presence in this crazy year of my life.

Thank you to my husband, Ron, for your support and unconditional love during this process. You graciously accept late dinners as part of the writing process.

My dear friend Kathie Keller has a special place in my heart. I lovingly recall the day we read my first attempts at writing. I thought she would be by my side during the journey, but it was not God's plan. Her initial encouragement was the confirmation I needed to step out in faith. If only she were here to see the book come to fruition.

My pastor, Mike Hailey and Debbie Boyd, for encouraging me to take the initial steps necessary to get off the fence and write. What better beginning to test the waters with my devotions than my home church?

Thank you to my sister Margaret for spending her vacations helping me edit my book rather than sunbathing at the beach. I couldn't have done it without you. I apologize for the late hours and the loss of sleep.

Kellie Stigliano inspired me to write and introduced me to Word Weavers. This entire group of writers is awesome. In addition, Kellie's available whenever I have a question regarding writing or publishing.

Katherine Hayes, Shari McGriff, and Jenifer Jennings thank you for the valuable writing insights. I need and appreciate friends with your expertise, willing to assist me.

Thanks to Judy Alexander for always coming to my aid whenever I have computer issues.

Lastly, I appreciate Covenant Books' patience and for giving me this opportunity.

1

Reverse the Lie

Lay not up for yourselves treasures upon earth, where moth and rust doth corrupt, and where thieves break through and steal: but lay up for yourselves treasures in heaven, where neither moth nor rust doth corrupt, and where thieves do not break through nor steal: for where your treasure is, there will your heart be also.
—Matthew. 6:19–21(KJV)

Devotional

Isolation is a blessing if you use it to heed God's promptings. It is a gift to be set apart with God for a time. However, some don't benefit from this time, just as some reject salvation. While we waste time, we could seek God. Those that realign priorities in their lives and implement the necessary changes draw close to God.

God allows solitude in our lives to reverse the lie that society accepts as truth. The myth of staying busy means you are productive when in actuality, nothing is more valuable than time in fellowship with God. The belief in entertainment bringing joy is a lie because it is a momentary pleasure that soon disappears. Only the Lord truly fulfills your life with everlasting joy. Security in wealth is a lie as it is subject to vanish tomorrow, and it doesn't bring happiness. Only God provides real riches that last an eternity.

When we trust Christ to guide us, we can lean firmly on him in uncertain times. Only then is our future secure. Most people, being finite creatures, think they are in control when in reality, none of us know what tomorrow will bring. Our wisdom and power are limited, but our infinite God can do all things and knows everything. He instructs us in his Word not to worry about tomorrow.

Many think what they believe is correct when ultimately, only God's truth is always correct. Times of isolation from others or even a more straightforward lifestyle without distractions allows more time to realize we desperately need the Lord and to turn our attention to him.

Reflect

What is essential to God?

CHOOSING CHRIST

Scriptures

John 8:31–32; 14:6
Jeremiah 29:13
Matthew 6:31–33

2

Out of Control

whereas ye know not what shall be on the
morrow. For what is your life? It is even
a vapour, that appeareth for a little time,
and then vanisheth away.

—James 4:14 (KJV)

Devotional

A season of government-mandated quarantines created emotions of depression, hopelessness, loneliness, uncertainty, and loss for many people. Although we had no control over the lack of work and the cancellation of all social activities, we still determined how we used the time available. It would be a blessing if this time when God's people were not allowed to gather in worship ushered in a spirit of restoration to God! Surely, it would make the church more focused, more united, and powerful because of the extra time Christians devoted to prayer.

No one knows what the future holds. When our thoughts are on tomorrow, we lose the opportunity to make a difference now. Live life one day at a time. It is not possible to always manage situations because life has a way of surprising us. We should plan for tomorrow with the understanding life can change quickly. When our heartfelt trust is in Christ, then our thoughts centered on understanding his Word produces hope. Hope does not disappoint. So our confidence is not in our well-made plans, but always our faith and belief are in God.

Our actions don't always influence our health, employment, wealth, or other people. Please don't allow a lack of power to create uncertainty, which leads to frustrations and worries that destroy our joy and peace. Trust in God; and remain calm by surrendering each day to the Lord, knowing he can provide more abundantly than we can imagine.

This quarantine season is a call for Christians to follow Christ boldly, selflessly love others, and genuinely show concern for others' eternity. Our actions as believers should bring others to the knowledge and acceptance of Christ. Rather than concentrating on circumstances beyond our ability, let's center on Christ's gift of love to his followers. It is a reminder to share our faith, his love, and pray for others. Let's thank God together for his protection during this season.

Reflect

How does surrendering your hopes and future to God bring freedom?

Scriptures

Proverbs 27:1
2 Chronicles 7:14
Hebrews 11:1

3

World Full of Anxiety

> Therefore I say unto you, Take no thought for your life, what ye shall eat, or what ye shall drink; nor yet for your body, what ye shall put on. Is not the life more than meat, and the body than raiment?
> —Matthew 6:25 (KJV)

Devotional

During my morning walk with a neighbor, the topic of conversation turns to the economy of our country and the world. All the advances in travel and technology are broader in recent years. We are no longer dependent on local products or seasonal produce. Global commerce makes a vast number of products easily accessible to us from around the world. It increases opportunities for growth because of an enlarged territory of operation. Simultaneously, we are much more dependent on other countries for the sale and purchase of products.

What is important to us as individuals if there are financial issues? Should we stockpile rations? After all, we should diligently provide for our families. We wrestle with these questions because we want to be ready. Picture a frightening world in which fear escalates due to the desire for self-preservation.

Will fear cause looting within our communities if hunger is rampant, or will the church reach out in love and share with others going without their basic needs? Will God miraculously multiply our limited supplies to accommodate the masses?

In 1 Kings 17, you will discover the story of Elijah. Through God's revelation, he declares to Ahab that there will be no rain for years, which will cause famine in the country. After he speaks, God leads Elijah to a brook and provides water and meat for him to eat. Later, God commands a widow to feed him. Throughout those days of famine, God supernaturally provides for Elijah. God will sustain us through times of disaster if we are walking in his will.

Reflect

How would God have you prepare for such an event?

Scriptures

Matthew 6:25–27
Philippians 4:19

4

Destructive Message

And why take ye thought for raiment? Consider the lilies of the field, how they grow; they toil not, neither do they spin: and yet I say unto you, That even Solomon in all his glory was not arrayed like one of these. Wherefore, if God so clothe the grass of the field, which today is, and tomorrow is cast into the oven, shall he not much more clothe you, O ye of little faith?

—Matthew 6:28–30 (KJV)

Devotional

Yesterday, as a friend and I walked through the neighborhood, the temperature dropped; and the wind increased. The dark, menacing clouds conveyed impending stormy weather was approaching our area. As we ended our walk, large pellets of rain began to fall. Driving rain battered a portion of our state throughout the night. Later in the evening, our favorite television show was interrupted by breaking news of severe weather conditions. This threatening weather broadcast continued for the remainder of the evening. The endless assault of doom reminded me of our current situation with the COVID-19 virus. Countless people are in despair since they have heard the same destructive message repeatedly pounded into their heads.

I realized the media-based headlines emphasized the worst possible outcome for their news reports. Of course, we should take reasonable safeguards to protect ourselves. The news headlines for the past several months have been negatively worded. Projections and even stats of deaths were inaccurate. Was it their purpose to instill fear in individuals to be afraid to leave their homes? But we do not need to live in fear as it robs us of today's joy and hope; however, God is the giver of peace. *John 14:27.*

Despite the forecast, our community awoke to a new and promising day. Praise the Lord!

I sit in the cool morning breeze, and I am most grateful to God. I look upon my garden glistening with a promise of new growth while the birds are resoundingly singing God's praise. I wonder how they manage to safely survive the onslaught of rain without the shelter we enjoy. Their song becomes music in my ears. Their chirruping confirms God's Word, which promises to shelter and provide for us just as he cares for the wildflowers and the birds.

Reflect

What burdens can you give to God in prayer because he cares for you?

Scriptures

Philippians 4:19
Philippians 4:6–9
1 Peter 5:7

5

Frantic

You are the light of the world. A town
built on a hill cannot be hidden. Neither
do people light a lamp and put it under a
bowl. Instead they put it on its stand, and
it gives light to everyone in the house. In
the same way, let your light shine before
others, that they may see your good deeds
and glorify your Father in heaven.
—Matthew 5:14–16 (NIV)

Devotional

My nightmare was an atmosphere full of hatred and dread,
with numerous individuals frightened for their lives.
Neighbors had fearfully hidden from their perpetrators in an
attempt to survive the atrocity. While the remaining people
were hysterically running searching for shelter and safety. It
was a place of total insanity where no one wanted to live. The

dream deceived me as I felt like a victim without an escape from the terror surrounding me.

The violence was inconceivable to someone who lived in a small, peaceful community in America. Thoughts of horror were nonexistent in our friendly little town. Undoubtedly, no one I know has seen the persecution many Christians endure on an almost daily basis. How could this happen here?

Terror was consuming me. It became challenging to breathe, and beads of sweat forms on my body. Panic was taking me into an unknown realm. How do you escape the extreme hatred that was increasing dread with each frantic breath? Erratic breathing created more urgency. It was challenging to determine if the heart was beating more vigorously and faster than the severe pain in my head. I lifted my hand to rub my face's painful side and felt the throbbing vein that had protruded. The veins were pulsing at a tremendous rate and intensity. The inflamed and swollen blood vessels vibrated pain with each step.

Suddenly I woke up. I sat on the bed in amazement. It was merely a dream. Every aspect of my entire being was full of dread and the human instinct for survival. My life had not changed, or was it forever different because the vision in my mind was surreal?

As Christians, the dream was all wrong because God made us in his image and likeness. It means we have the authority and power of Christ to shine brightly, not hide. What a revelation. My entire dream wrongly focused on myself when my focus should have been on God and his will for my life! We can't hide his love; if we do, we miss his purpose for our lives.

We, as Christians, walk in his divine power and are not led by our emotions. Was this dream merely a nightmare or a revelation from God of a concern to be confronted? Had the devil attempted to plant a seed of anxiety to immobilize me as a Christian? The dream revealed to not depend upon emotions but to submit to his purpose for your life. It validated a desire to witness to others the love of God.

Acts of eternal value are more important than comfort and circumstances. God walks through these times with us, giving us strength so our future is secure. Our victory is in him!

Reflect

Evaluate your witness during trials; in what ways do your actions and words reveal God's love towards others?

Scriptures

2 Timothy 1:7
James 1:12
1 Corinthians 10:13

6

World Ablaze

> Nevertheless we, according to his prom-
> ise, look for new heavens and a new earth,
> wherein dwelleth righteousness.
> —2 Peter 3:13 (KJV)

Devotional

While relaxing in an atmosphere of calm reflection, I feel the
Spirit of God in the soft breeze, the repetition of the soothing
waves, and the clouds' movement. My thoughts are of God's
plan for the world and all human beings. God desires for each
individual to have a relationship with him. He is the great I
AM! He always existed—he is today and will be forever. When
we follow Christ's plan for our future, then life is rewarding.

We decide whether or not to follow his promptings.

I hear unfamiliar music flowing from a nearby neighbor's radio. The lyrics which catch my attention are about
the world ablaze. I scan the beautiful world around me, and I

suddenly remember this world will cease one day. Revelation speaks of judgment and desolation of the earth. Fire will consume it. We do not know when his holy judging will occur, but God tells us that no man—not even his Son, Jesus—discerns the day or hour he will return. Just verdicts will follow his return. However, as Christians, this book prepares us for the end of this world and a new earth. It is a glimpse of the future, which includes both warnings and glorious promises regarding end times. Our future is hopeful of eternity with the Lord. Praise be to God that he will create a new heaven and a new earth.

> And I saw a new heaven and a new earth:
> for the first heaven and the first earth
> were passed away; and there was no more
> sea.
> —Revelation 21:1 (KJV)

Reflect

Imagine the splendor of God dwelling with us in the new earth. Consider the magnitude of a world without death, mourning, weeping, pain, or darkness. What emotion does your meditation evoke?

Scriptures

Revelation 8:5–10
Revelation 20:15
Revelation 21:1–7
Isaiah 65:17–19

7

Cracks

For if, when we were enemies, we were
reconciled to God by the death of his
Son, much more, being reconciled, we
shall be saved by his life.
—Romans 5:10 (KJV)

Devotional

While strolling through our subdivision, I noticed a crevice in
the sidewalk where the grass is forcing itself through the soil
between cement sections. Suddenly I am contemplating all
sorts of gaps in our world and the fact we are always attempt-
ing to fill those cavities or empty spaces. Grave situations in
our lives reveal the absence of the Holy Spirit within us. We
are incapable of getting rid of the voids without him. Our
creator designs vacuums to appeal to our desire for fullness
in him. God allows us the liberty to choose whether we yearn

for him or not. When we try to grasp the unfathomable love of God, then he fills us with a portion of his passion.

However, when we fill the hollowness with things that do not meet our most profound need to know him, our lives feel meaningless. Searching for activities, individuals, experiences, self-medications, or places will not satisfy the yearnings within us. They will eventually bring bondage, addiction, and increasing pain.

On the other hand, disciplines, like quiet times for conversing with God, foster a closer relationship with God and reap eternal benefits.

Just as any athlete, we must train our bodies in the obedience of godly habits. Our flesh will not initially find it enjoyable, but the lasting profits far surpass the pain.

Filling the voids in your life with more of God is a gratifying journey to the richness of life.

Reflect

Are you continually searching for something missing from your life? If so, how could you develop a deeper relationship with Christ?

Scriptures

1 Corinthians 9:26–27
Ephesians 3:14–21
Matthew 6:24
Hebrews 11:1; 12:11

8

Hope and Expectation

> Then young women will dance and be
> glad, young men and old as well. I will turn
> their mourning into gladness; I will give
> them comfort and joy instead of sorrow.
> —Jeremiah 31:13 (NIV)

Devotional

When my daughter was only two, I became pregnant. My dream was to raise twins because of a family history of twins on my mom's side. My eyes sparkled, and my face lit up with a smile when the doctor announced their forthcoming arrival. The feeling of joy and expectation I experienced was incredible. Then four months into my pregnancy, my water broke; after several weeks in the hospital, I came home, but I was on complete bed rest. My mother brought me a book about miracles. I filled long and endless days reading and seeking God in prayer. I looked forward to carrying the twins to term.

As the doctor delivered my child, he held the first-born precious tiny baby up for me to see. My beloved son's petite body brought tears to my eyes because it was difficult to distinguish the little fingers from each other, even at an extremely short distance. A fragile infant cradled in the palm of the physician's hand.

How could such a tiny body be so wonderfully formed to the smallest detail?

He gently handed the baby to a nurse, then pulled the sheet over my head to prevent me from seeing the second of our baby boys delivered. The next moments lacked the doctor presenting a perfect baby. There was a weird sensation; something was wrong and emptiness invaded me. Later the doctor came to my bedside as they wheeled me from the delivery room with the earthshattering news that neither of the twins was alive. I had seen the beautifully formed body of the first child, so I couldn't grasp the reality of his words. My twins were birthed and died too quickly for me even to cradle them in my arms.

When I unexpectedly went into labor at six months, my hope and expectation were for a miracle. After all, God is good; and he only wants the best for me, right? Small hospitals during the early 1970s did not have the technology we now enjoy. The survival of twins born three months premature would have been a miraculous occurrence. Instead of experiencing the supernatural, we returned home without our miracle babies.

Tasks such as disassembling the nursery and storing all their little clothes seemed insurmountable. While working through my grief, I expressed my feelings in a letter to God. The only comforting fact was the knowledge our twins were in heaven. Jesus was the first one to hold them in a tight embrace.

Only mere moments after birth, they arrived in heaven and were in the arms of Jesus and obtained what we hope for God to bring to completion for us. They heard Jesus welcome them to heaven, which is every Christian's goal.

We desire to persevere and remain devoted throughout our lives. Several weeks later, the mailman delivered a live birth certificate along with two death certificates for our babies. The live birth documentation threw me into despair; however, the letter that I had written to the Lord, acknowledging our babies' forever home with Jesus, served as my anchor. It was evident that they were both in a better place.

One of the twins' death caused my body to abort the other infant before it was strong enough to survive. This miscarriage was the first of three I endured between the births of my two daughters. They were difficult times because I felt God was blessing us with a child. Each loss unquestionably tested my faith. After every hurt, I asked God over and over again *why* and *what if.* God could have, in an instant, made them healthy and whole, but he chose not to. If I only knew the answer to my questions. I finally realized that even if God responded to my questions, it would be impossible to truly comprehend his reply as his purposes are infinitely more complex than earthly matters. Life and death are a part of our lives. This season taught me to lean on the goodness of our Heavenly Father through failure and hardship. Who am I to demand anything from God?

> For as the heavens are higher than the earth, so are my ways higher than your ways, and my thoughts than your thoughts. (Isa. 55:9 KJV)

Reflect

Think of a time you did not receive the answer you expected from God; did you understand why not? How did God comfort and assure you of his love?

Scriptures

Psalms 126:5
2 Corinthians 7:10
Job 2:10

9

Dazed After a Loss

Why art thou cast down, O my soul?
And why art thou disquieted within me?
Hope thou in God: for I shall yet praise
him, who is the health of my counte-
nance, and my God.

—Psalm 42:11 (KJV)

Devotional

Often during times of grief, I suffered in a daze of confusion. Each of us has lost a person we love. The death was
unreal because we were emotionally incapable of handling
the torment acceptance would bring. Heartache and misery
on earth have always been real, and a normal part of life. The
anguish of loss has remained a part of the grieving process
for most people. God placed this natural coping mechanism
within our bodies to gradually come to terms with our loss.

God was with me as I turned to him; he carried me through the difficult days. I rejoiced in him because my strength, hope, and joy were in him. How do I help others when mere words are inadequate?

No doubt, you have felt a state of denial was the only way you could cope with the hardships in life? You were devastated by the passing of someone you love. You suffered in shock, and at the moment, the only way you were capable of dealing with it was to isolate yourself from the pain by refusing to acknowledge the loss. You preferred to be in a trance instead of forcing yourself to accept reality. The numbness helped you appear in control of your feelings when you have little power over your emotions.

This disbelief gave a false sense of relief from sorrow when our refuge and security are only in God. Turn to God for help accepting your loss and acknowledging your need for his healing touch to strengthen you.

Reflect

Reflect on the promises in Christ of a joyful heavenly home. How does it change your grief?

Scriptures

Habakkuk 3:17–18
Romans 12:12
Psalm 46:1
Psalm 126:5
Revelation 21:4

Finality and Eternity

Jesus said unto her, I am the resurrection, and the life: he that believeth in me,
though he were dead, yet shall he live:
and whosoever liveth and believeth in me
shall never die. Believest thou this?
                    —John 11:25–26 (KJV)

Devotional

The sprawling hospice building is a maze of sterile hallways
and numerous rooms on both sides of the corridor. I ner-
vously hurry down the hall in pursuit of my mom. The faces
of most of the people I encounter have solemn expressions.
Even the workers have serious demeanors. There isn't the
usual workplace chitchat. Drawing closer to my destination,
the more disquieted my emotions become. I approach the
door and take a deep breath as my hand reaches for the door-
knob. I push the door open, bracing myself, I am exhaling

in relief when my eyes catch a glimpse of Mom propped up against pillows on the bed. She is enjoying the bright sunlight and beautiful clouds through the sparkling windowpane. We each smile lovingly at the other thankful for another day.

Nursing homes and hospitals are incredibly emotional for me because they are gloomy. I feel the pain of others terribly. Sickness and death are an almost daily occurrence and are not a respecter of people; even the very young and healthy can become casualties.

I'm confident that none of us wish to endure an agonizing death. In reality, there are situations that a person may prefer to die rather than burden loved ones or to hurt continuously. Death is final and may not end all suffering, but it ends all opportunity to accept Jesus's grace and forgiveness. Our earthly death ushers us into eternity—in either heaven or hell. It is incomprehensible for us to conceive eternity in the endlessness of torment and suffering.

The good news is that our heavenly Father loves all of us, and his desire is for all to accept eternal life with him in paradise. He prepared the way for us by sending his Son, who paid the penalty for our sins. We have eternal salvation through Jesus Christ, our Savior. Living a life for Jesus is rewarding here on earth and in eternity. Yes, we will continue to have trials in this world, but he walks with us through them. When we are weary and weak, we lean on him for strength.

He brings peace amid troubles. He provides for our daily needs.

We can joyfully imagine the glory of life in heaven. When I envision heaven, Jesus is so majestic that he captivates the attention of everyone. All the saints are completely awestruck; nothing else can compete with the wonder of him. Jesus is The Light; as Revelation tells us, his glory is exceedingly radiant. He is our endless source of light, and it is brilliant. His brilliance and radiance are pure in form without flaw. He is pure beyond our comprehension.

Reflect

Meditate on what the Good News of Jesus means to you and how you would relay the gospel message to someone who inquires?

Scriptures

Romans 3:23–24; 5:8; 6:23
Luke 16:19–31

11

Armor

Put on the whole armor of God, that ye may be able to stand against the wiles of the devil. For we wrestle not against flesh and blood, but against principalities, against powers, against the rulers of the darkness of this world, against spiritual wickedness in high places.

—Ephesians 6:11–12 (KJV)

Devotional

I occasionally use melatonin when unable to sleep. Regretfully, it is the cause of vivid dreams. I suddenly wake up from a deep sleep with the grave need to put on the armor of God. Although it is invisible, there is a heaviness of doom. A dark, threatening cloud is descending upon me, so I wonder about its origin and its meaning.

Due to the disturbing presence of evil surrounding me; keen awareness of a spiritual battle and the need to protect myself from Satan's tactics overpower me. I pray to the Lord about my concerns while visualizing clothing myself with each piece of God's armor, our defense to stand against the devil. Moments later, I open my Bible to Ephesians to read the entire scripture, which not only speaks of the armor.

I am familiar with the scripture about arming yourself for battle, but the sentence includes additional instruction to pray in the Spirit. The Word of God is enlightening me to pray in the Spirit because it is a pertinent part of our defense. He teaches us all things if we ask him. Quite honestly, I need to pray in the Spirit more often and devote enough time to memorizing the scripture. Do I know enough scripture to defend myself against the devil without the Bible at my side? The devil knows the Bible in-depth as he is a fallen angel. He questioned God regarding Job's devotion to him, and he tried to tempt Jesus in the wilderness.

The armor of God is our valuable resource. The Bible instructs us always to remain ready for spiritual warfare, ask the Lord what we should do to equip ourselves against evil in this world. We fight the enemy by knowing and declaring God's written Word. We prepare by hiding his Word in our hearts. Devoting more time to study and memorize scriptures related to the armor will please God and ensure we are ready for battle.

Reflect

Is it imperative to have all pieces of the armor of God during spiritual battles? What would be the result if one is missing?

Scriptures

Isaiah 61:10
Ephesians 6:14–18
John 14:26

12

Eternal Assurance

Though you have not seen him, you love him; and even though you do not see him now, you believe in him and are filled with an inexpressible and glorious joy.

—1 Peter 1:8 (NIV)

Devotional

The truth is many things can occur without warning and catch us off guard, and we realize we are not in control. Regardless of how proactive we prepare, things happen we do not anticipate. For example, you eat healthily and exercise but receive a cancer diagnosis. None of us have control of all situations, and we have no idea when the unforeseen will blindside us.

There is an unforeseen event, not within our control—losing a dear friend following a short illness. Her death had upset my life.

We have no clue what will happen each day we are here on earth. However, there is a way to be confidently anticipating eternity with God in the future. My friend knew Lord Jesus as her Savior. I take comfort in the assurance angels are singing and rejoicing while my friend is at rest. She prepared for eternity.

You can prepare for that moment in your life as well. Say yes to Jesus's gift of forgiveness and eternal life. Unfortunately, all of us are guilty of sin.

Is he Lord of your life? The term means Jesus has first place in your life, so live a life to please him. Let his Spirit guide and transform you. Live a life of righteousness honoring him. When you have faith in Christ, God promises you eternal life with him in heaven.

Nothing can compare to the blessed assurance and love, which will abound as we serve the Lord. But what exactly does *peace* mean? It is tranquility or quiet freedom from troubling thoughts or emotions. Many things, both internally and externally, rob us of calmness. But God gives us peace which surpasses all understanding. God's serenity allows us to remain still, calm, and restful, regardless of our circumstances. God is not the author of confusion, so when you feel confused, recognize the need to ask God for help.

His goodness and mercy are beyond description. Faith in God creates awe and confidence in his supremacy. Trust him with everything because nothing is impossible for God—this belief imparts a consuming peace within you.

There is nothing like giving the Lord your burdens, allowing the Creator of the universe to guide you.

Reflect

Because of Jesus' willing death we have the opportunity to be pardoned. He hates sin but endured it for us. Have you said yes to the Lord? If you have accepted Jesus, spread the good news to others by sharing your story of when you accepted Christ as your Savior.

OR

If you wish to invite Jesus into your life, see the book's back portion for a prayer of salvation. The prayer cannot save you. Your salvation comes from the Lord when you put your faith in him and his Word. He promises salvation to all who believe.

Scriptures

1 John 1:7
Matthew 6:33
Romans 10:10
1 Peter 3:15

13

Bold Confidence

For I know that this shall turn to my salvation through your prayer, and the supply of the Spirit of Jesus Christ, according to my earnest expectation and my hope, that in nothing I shall be ashamed, but that with all boldness, as always, so now also Christ shall be magnified in my body, whether it be by life, or by death.
—Philippians 1:19–20 (KJV)

Devotional

Most of us feel we have control of situations giving us a false sense of self-reliance. No one wants to feel helpless and at the mercy of another. Even our well-thought-out plans often change abruptly. Of course, we plan for tomorrow but with the understanding that circumstances over which we are powerless can quickly change today and our future forever.

Something may happen tomorrow which turns life in an unexpected direction, destroying our plans.

Earthly things are subject to change or disappear from our lives. What we possess today may be gone tomorrow. Therefore, our confidence is in God rather than the uncontrollable temporal things. Only God is constant in our lives because he is still the same every day and will never leave us. God is ultimately in control; we can place our confidence in his Word and promises. Worrying about the future causes us to lose the opportunity to make an impact now. So live life one day at a time, and give your concerns about tomorrow to Christ.

This quarantine makes us aware of how swiftly our job status, freedom, and lifestyle are apt to change. It is a wakeup call as followers of Christ to cherish each day, selflessly show love toward others, and be sincerely concerned about the eternity of others. We do decide our actions as believers. Rather than concentrating on circumstances beyond our control, we can choose to focus our efforts on things of eternal value by making the most of every opportunity given us to share our love of Christ. If every Christian's priority is living a life pleasing God, this world would be a marvelous place.

In gratitude for God's mercy and grace, let us show others the forgiveness and love Christ bestows on us. When we share and pray with or for others, we fulfill our call as

Christians. The opportunity to lead others to the knowledge and acceptance of Christ is the highest of honors. Evangelism is a discipline we should develop. Be prepared at all times to give our testimony.

Reflect

Consider and list how you can lovingly and boldly proclaim your faith in difficult times.

Scriptures

Luke 12:20–21
James 4:13–17
Proverbs 27:1
Hebrews 4:14–16

14

Treasure Each Day

But he was wounded for our transgressions, he was bruised for our iniquities: the chastisement of our peace was upon him; and with his stripes we are healed.
—Isaiah 53:5 (KJV)

Devotional

Regardless of the circumstances, be thankful for the day. Many individuals are in a battle for their lives; they are grateful for the most challenging of situations. They smile over the smallest of triumphs. One more day of hardship is a win— even if it is a long day full of grueling prods, tests, and pain. A thankful heart brings hope in dire times.

I remember well our suffering when our eldest grandchild was battling a cancerous brain tumor. She was a young teen of thirteen years of age. She did not have the usual frustrations, such as excessive peer pressure. Her concerns were not just whether she was well-liked, beautiful, or intelligent. Her burdens were whether or not she would survive the treatment without brain damage. She struggled to cope with an unexpected diagnosis and emergency operation.

Later, hospital stays, daily doctor visits, blood work, treatments, extreme weakness, loss of appetite, relentless nausea, loss of friends, separation from family members, baldness, was her new life away from home. Even so, she was thankful for her mom always beside her, a successful operation, positive results from treatments, prayers of many faithful church members, and the few friends who remain loyal to this day. Ronald McDonald's house was a huge blessing as their home away from home.

God intervened in a situation where the doctor's recommendation could have resulted in harm. God again interceded, and she received proton treatment at UNF. The list of blessings was enormous. These included a loving home for her younger brother plus a loaned vehicle during out-of-state treatments. After the treatments, my daughter could not find employment, and they needed a place to live. A couple within their church welcomed them into their home. God sent many incredible people into their lives.

Anyone who loves someone with a dreadful, life-threatening disease has so many conflicting emotions. Yet, we wish to take their sickness upon ourselves and shelter them from both pain and harm. We feel helpless and must depend upon doctors' opinions. Doctors are marvelous, but they are only human. Physicians have the opportunity to present probabilities in a manner that instills hope. Our hope each day is from the Lord. He can provide more abundantly than any person.

I am thankful our family loves the Lord and had the incredible support of Christian friends who believe in the power of prayer for the impossible. Nothing is impossible for God. Our direction, peace, strength, and healing all come from the Lord. Before the medical test confirmed our grandchild's recovery, God assured me deep within my spirit; all is well with both my daughter and granddaughter. God's courage and strength are evident within each of them. Their tremendous confidence in Jesus for both complete healing and his assurance of everlasting life brought me joy.

Praise God she is alive and well more than a decade later! We are beyond thankful for each year with her. This period of our lives is a reminder to cherish each day. Every new day is a gift from God and is so very precious. Although I sometimes fail in this regard, I try not to take any day for granted and always spend it wisely. Treasure each day of life with those you love as each day is the most precious of gifts.

Reflect

Let us make a list of the things we are thankful for today.

> Rejoice always, pray continually, give thanks in all circumstances; for this is God's will for you in Christ Jesus. (1 Thessalonians 5:16-18 NIV)

Scriptures

2 Corinthians 12:9
John 14:27
John 10:28

15

Hyphen

I have fought a good fight, I have finished my course, I have kept the faith: henceforth there is laid up for me a crown of righteousness, which the Lord, the righteous judge, shall give me at that day: and not to me only, but unto all them also that love his appearing.

—2 Timothy 4:7–8 (KJV)

Devotional

I looked at the marble tombstone on my grandfather's plot within the old cemetery grounds. My thoughts went to the brevity of the date-dash-date. I had walked through the cemetery to see whose body lay beneath the different monuments. Does what was inscribed on the marker accurately reflect their contribution to society? Does their epitaph fully describe their life? How could a dash accurately reflect the value of one's existence? It was as if the tiny insignificant-looking hyphen summed up the entirety of a person's triumphs, with one placed between their birth and death.

I imagine in the scope of eternity; our lives are simple dashes—perhaps so minuscule the time is a dot or dash. Our lives are as a second in eternity. In a flash, it is over and it appears life is too short even to make an impact on anyone. Our lives on earth are more important than we will ever comprehend while living. At the final judgment, we will suddenly be fully aware of how many precious moments we wasted. The mere thought of it brings me sorrow as I am most likely among the biggest offenders.

All of us have the same hours each day. Every day has potential either for good, evil, or waste. The number of days that we have on earth is unknown. Many things require daily attention to keep the physical body, mind, and spirit healthy. It is a delicate dance of balancing work, study, prayer, rest, nourishment, sleep, relationships, and recreation to focus on essential matters in the proper perspective.

Most of us have periods in life where there are not enough hours in our day for all demands and pressures. A person must deliberately hone in on the things essential for that season. Seasons change as time passes. Often, what we do today will impact our future. Without prayerful planning, today, and tomorrow, we may bring unnecessary self-inflicted anguish and suffering.

When your time on earth is almost over isn't the best time to realize you have little of value to show for it. Regularly examining your innermost thoughts and motives will keep you from falling away from the Lord. Reflect upon God's purpose for you to determine any actions you can make to accomplish his plan. God gives us a deep hunger in our souls that only his presence can satisfy. When we let his Spirit into those places, we become whole and holy!

Reflect

Will the simple hyphen on your tombstone represent a complete and well-lived life? Write an epitaph that reflects your life and inspires future generations to a life of love and service to the Lord.

Scriptures

1 Corinthians 9:25
2 Timothy 4:7–8
Hebrews 12:1–2
Romans 13:10

16

Miry Mud

He brought me up also out of an horrible
pit, out of the miry clay, And set my feet
upon a rock, and established my goings.
—Psalms 40:2 (KJV)

Devotional

Even the miry mud along the shoreline has a small stream of
water flowing toward it, which transforms into the appear-
ance of glitter. The sun's intense rays touching the moist soil
turn the sludge into a sparkling surprise. Behold the hand
of God, scattering the glittery light from his sun across the
earth. The shimmering mud is God's way of speaking hope
into the lives of those who have the eyes to see the light.

Open your eyes to the majesty of God and the breath-
taking beauty of his creation. Let the evidence of his existence soak into your innermost being. Allow your eyes to
open your heart to whatever God reveals to you. He offers

hope in the unkindness of life's situations. You merely need to accept his gifts of creation, such as the sun and his most precious gift—the offering of his Son, Jesus Christ! Then he will fill you with love for all people.

When we allow the light from God's only Son, Jesus Christ, to rest upon us and touch our lives, he changes us into his loving image. Do you want to be made into the image of God? Slowly his refreshing water flows within us. His water gives our thirsty souls a drink of the living water we are searching for in various ways or things.

Our very being catches a spark of hope, and as faith increases, joy ignites within us. Jesus is the light of the world. His sacrificial love draws people to him. Let the light of your love shine so that others come to Christ!

Reflect

Think about how you can fill this dark world with your brightly shining light, so your confidence in God radiates to all who cross your path.

Scriptures

Ephesians 5:8
Matthew 5: 16; 6:22–23
John 3:19
1 Corinthians 6:2

17

Chirping

Take therefore no thought for the morrow: for the morrow shall take thought for the things of itself. Sufficient unto the day is the evil thereof.

—Matthew 6:34 (KJV)

Devotional

It is early in the morning, shortly before the dawn of a new day. Everything is quiet and peaceful because there is no activity outside. Several weeks under quarantine, which is an attempt to halt the spread of a deadly virus, feels more like months. There is no longer the typical noise of children and parents as they go about their days full of activities and obligations. Most people are behind walls and closed doors unless necessity forces them from their homes. When out, they are behind a face mask or caringly practicing social distancing.

No one previously knew of social distancing, much less anyone willingly practicing it. The world is ever-changing, and some things we cannot control. Even the usual activities of gathering for church services or celebrations of life, such as weddings, graduations, and funerals, have ceased. There certainly is no entertainment. Laughter and shouts of happiness at sports events and all other community gatherings are in our recent past.

As I sit listening to the beautiful sound of birds singing, their constant tweeting brings gladness and normalcy back into my life. All the chirping is coming from dozens of baby birds. They must be everywhere. How delightfully they are welcoming the new day. It sparks thankfulness and hope within my spirit. Each day is an occasion to worship Christ. His Word instructs us to live each day to the fullest and not worry about tomorrow as tomorrow will take care of itself. There is not a more accurate statement.

You cannot add to tomorrow by worrying about today. You only waste today in defeat. So smile at the birds, and sing to the Lord along with them. God blesses your day so that you may bless others in return. Everything is beautiful. Spread your joy to others.

Fill in the extra hours you unknowingly receive due to the canceled activities with actions of love. Love creates gladness in both you and the recipient. Find joy in all circumstances or make all your moments joyful—phone or text, a friend with a thankful heart that God has that person in your life. Give God the glory for his goodness! Live purposefully for him by praying for others and genuinely loving others.

Reflect

What causes joy to rise in you regardless of your circumstances? How does the joy of the Lord differ from the world's happiness?

Scriptures

1 Thessalonians 5:16–18
1 Peter 1:8
Romans 14:17

18

A Good Friday Memory

"He himself bore our sins" in his body on
the cross, so that we might die to sins and
live for righteousness; "by his wounds
you have been healed."
—1 Peter 2:24 (NIV)

Devotional

My husband decided to paint the outside of our house on
Good Friday many years ago. I expressed my concern about
the scaffolding he was using. Rather than watch him, I walked
over to our next-door neighbor's home and was in the middle of a conversation. Terror immediately struck me when
I heard the massive crash from our home's vicinity. Dread
washed over me in a wave as I hurriedly rounded the corner
of our dwelling.

One day, he was walking, and the next day, he was
undergoing surgery. The surgeon advised us Ron would
never walk normally again, and recommended that I help my

husband accept this fact by not giving him the false hope of doing anything that required walking or standing.

We depended on God daily and saw countless miracles of provision. Ron lived with pain and walked with a cane for years. Seven years later, a dear friend told him about a natural fruit juice, which was considered a "gift of God" by generations of Pacific Islanders. God used this person to answer Ron's need regarding his pain. This exceptional fruit juice has healing properties and was a gift from God because Ron walks free of any pain or a walking cane.

All my thoughts of this incident are thanks and praise to God. God protected my husband as it could have been a deadly crash. He also enabled his healing and freedom from pain and provided for our needs during this time of recovery.

Reflect

What do you believe regarding God's perfect timing and divine healing?

Scriptures

2 Kings 20:5
Jeremiah 30:17
First Peter 2:24

19

Baby Girl Trauma

Therefore, if anyone is in Christ, the new
creation has come: The old has gone, the
new is here!
>   —2 Corinthians 5:17 (NIV)

Devotional

I find the fall weather is rejuvenating, but it brings to my
mind a horrifying memory. Portions of one particular
Halloween night are vivid in my mind even though it has
been many years since the incident. We took our two young
daughters to a fall festival at our public school. The usual
activities with various games, costumes of all kinds, and
regular carnival food delighted all the young children. We
maneuvered through the crowds with our hands, clasping the
girls as children laughed and screamed with pleasure.

Shortly before the judging of costumes began, I lifted
my adorable little two-year-old, dressed as a clown, onto the

platform, and she timidly stood there. As I watched my baby girl, an awful expression came over her face. A thick layer of white clown paint on her innocent face did not disguise the anguish. Chubby baby arms reached out to me. I thought she was nauseous. I ran and lifted her in my arms, then rushed across the gym floor toward the bathroom. I struggled to keep a firm grasp on her limp body. Suddenly, I realized her severe condition, the fear she was dead overcame me as eyes rolled behind their sockets, and her head swung around and backward.

I frantically prayed to God that she would live, and I ran aimlessly, unsure which direction to go for help. Then I pushed open the bathroom door to escape the busy hallway. I gently eased my baby onto the floor. While bent over her body, someone entered the room, stared, and then rushed out to find help. Right away, an EMT working the event entered and at once checked for a pulse and began CPR on her lifeless body as I stood in shock. Praise God, she revived! We hastily made necessary arrangements for our seven-year-old to stay with a friend while we quickly jumped into the vehicle with our toddler.

We lived over sixty miles away from the closest hospital, so the EMT drove at max speed. Our little angel remained unresponsive to the prayers and loving words I spoke during the drive. Anxiously, I watched my daughter's beautiful face for a change, but blank eyes stared back. There was no spark of light indicating awareness. My silent cry was, "Is she blind or unconscious?" She was lifelessly still and unaware of her surroundings. Waving my hand across her face brought no responsiveness in her gaze. She was not conscious or could not see my hand. Before we arrived at the hospital, she began to improve and slowly gained awareness. The medical staff examined and observed her behavior, and later, she was released with instructions to see a pediatric cardiologist at the children's hospital. She was later diagnosed with an atrial septal defect. She had a hole between the top two heart chambers.

During the drive home, it was impossible to restrain our toddler without a car seat. No, we were not breaking the law as car seats were not mandatory in 1977. She refused to sit still; instead, she crawled and climbed everywhere. It was the behavior of a typically energetic and curious toddler. The transformation, over a few short but agonizing hours, was astounding. We are grateful she had a normal childhood with no other incidents. Praises to God for his saving and transforming hand, restoring life!

When you give your life to the Lord, attitudes and desires are different as the relationship with him deepens. You are spiritually altered into the likeness of God when yielded to the Lord in obedience. The conversion from lost to devoted Christian is astonishing. God's amazing grace is transforming.

Reflect

Write a story about the changes within you after your conversion.

Scriptures

Titus 3:4–6

20

Open or Closed

I will give you a new heart and put a
new spirit in you; I will remove from you
your heart of stone and give you a heart
of flesh.

—Ezekiel 36:26 (NIV)

Devotional

During the more relaxed spring nights, we sleep with our
bedroom windows open. Morning's bright light enters the
room through the window, bathing us in the warmth of its
rays. The cheerful sound of birds singing with glee while
the sun lights up the eastern sky brings joy. It doesn't matter
whether the birds are battered by rain all night; the dark of
night is quickly in their past. Their happy chatter for another
day full of possibilities is a reminder for us to wake up with
gratitude in our hearts. Their chirps arouse happiness and joy

as the birds' melody ushers in songs of praise to the Lord for another beautiful day.

Now our windows are shut due to the extreme summer heat. It is as if the weather and the virus create a conspiracy against us. Closed shops and windows produce a sense of being cut off from the world. No longer do we wake up to the sweet melody of birds. The absence of happy sounds creates feelings of isolation.

There is little traffic in the stores and restaurants, no laughter from children playing in the streets. A sinister silence abounds. Closed signs are typical due to the Coronavirus. Some shop owners, without the expectation of survival, are no longer in business. The empty buildings look forsaken.

What a bleak reminder of how little the world has to offer us because there is no vision or future without the hope of God. It isn't easy to make it through life without faith. Our confidence is in Christ because he is our answer. He brings hope to the living and assurance of eternal life. Eternity with Christ is the ultimate of all his promises.

Open your heart to embrace a bright new day full of God's promises. Allow the brilliant sunrise to dismiss doom, just as the light of Christ illuminates the world. A gentle breeze stirs the air and lifts the sound of peace and joy to the heavens as the refreshing winds of revival chase away silence and proclaim the resounding power of almighty God.

The Lord walks with us; no matter what happens, his presence and love reside in us. His Spirit brings us safely through the darkness into his marvelous light. We never travel through this world alone because his Holy Spirit lives in all who accept and believe. Don't face another day alone; seek him.

Reflect

Consider ways your heart is open or closed to Christ today.

Scriptures

Psalm 51:10
Proverbs 3:5–6, 4:23

21

Each Beat Becomes
a Melody

> Do not be anxious about anything, but
> in every situation, by prayer and petition,
> with thanksgiving, present your requests to
> God. And the peace of God, which tran-
> scends all understanding, will guard your
> hearts and your minds in Christ Jesus.
> —Philippians 4:6–7 (NIV)

Devotional

Ron is lying close to my side. It is disquieting because I feel
the beat of a heart. My head isn't resting on his chest, so I am
confused. Could my heart be racing? If not, I feel more alarm.
Is it possible for me to feel his heartthrob so strongly? At that
moment, the beat seems almost audible, as if it is pounding.
It isn't racing but appears to be exceptionally forceful. Could

his blood pressure be elevated? Various fearful thoughts begin to go through my mind. While pondering the possibility of a health problem, it becomes difficult to relax. The continuous thoughts keep me from falling asleep, so I lay in bed, listening, in an attempt to detect a health issue. I then ask God for peace as my husband seems to be in a restful state. I am lying in the stillness, concentrating my thoughts on worship songs to Christ. I start to relax, realizing his breathing is normal and not strenuous. Ron is at peace, quietly sleeping while I allow thoughts to rob me of peace.

Soon the rhythm of his heart comforts and reassures me. It brings the peace I so desire. Each beat becomes a melody in my heart as it assures me he is alive. The slow, steady beat turns into a blessed dance tune to my ears. Thankful for my husband's presence in my life, I drift off to sleep. Gratitude consumes my heart because every breath of life and moment with those I love is precious.

So often, we allow fearful thoughts to rob our life of joy. The devil comes to destroy our peace, but Christ has come to give us peace and abundant joy. We have victory because we know real peace comes only from God. His words tell us to think about good thoughts and always to be thankful.

Reflect

What fearful thoughts from Satan have you entertained which destroyed your peace?

Scriptures

John 10:10
2 Peter 1:2
Romans 15:13

22

Hospital Visit

For the Spirit God gave us does not make
us timid, but gives us power, love and
self-discipline.

—2 Timothy 1:7 (NIV)

Devotional

I visited my friend in the hospital. A sign instructed visitors to see the nurse before entering the room. The nurse informed me that if I felt sick, I needed to wear a mask. I felt fine, so I did not ask for a surgical mask.

We had a great visit. During our conversation, we spoke about being worriers at times. I told her my husband had given me a book for Christmas, *Prayer Worrier*. It was a discouraging gift for a Christian to receive a book about praying while continuing to worry rather than releasing the problem to the Lord.

My explanation was, "I am a thinker and am proactive, but I don't keep thinking about things." Later during the day, my throat felt a little sore. Even though I did not have a fever, I found myself earnestly worried about my friend and that I might be contagious. It was a battle in prayer to God to protect and heal my friend during the middle of the night. My prayers were that his sweet Holy Spirit would fill her room so all evil would flee. I called my prayer partners to declare a hedge of protection around my friend, no germ, infection, and illness can penetrate. A team of believers claimed complete healing for my friend's body and freedom from fear for me as I had allowed myself to become fearful. I felt terrible, emotionally. The next day, I discovered my friend had fought fever until early morning.

Often, we recognize the truth after our trials. The devil devised evil for my friend and me, but God intervened, and it was a time of praying and crying to God for my dear friend. Praise be to God. We are both at peace. Sometimes we must stand our ground against Satan.

Reflect

When you have fearful thoughts, how do you defeat them?

Scriptures

Matthew 6:34
1 Peter 2:24

23

In Plain Sight

My prayer is not that you take them out of the world but that you protect them from the evil one. They are not of the world, even as I am not of it. Sanctify them by the truth; your word is truth. As you sent me into the world, I have sent them into the world.

—John 17:15–18 (NIV)

Devotional

When I sat down to read the Bible one morning, my glasses were missing from where I usually sat to study. I scanned the room and looked in the areas I generally placed them, but I could not find them. So I returned to the bedroom. It was the average-size bedroom with a tiny little reading nook. My eyes moved from one piece of furniture to another, intently focusing on each in search of my glasses; at last, I discovered them. I first thought they were on the bedside table in plain view, but I didn't realize it because both were the same color. But then, I wondered how often I failed to notice things?

The world is different from past years because of escalating fears, hatred, and division. Some evil is easily visible, while others are less apparent due to hidden agendas and motives. Perhaps the world is more complex and not as innocent as I perceived. Did the unusual circumstances of recent months make me more aware of the mounting evil and the need to test the spirits?

I believe people are honest and truthful until I discover otherwise. Now I wonder if accepting something as real without proof is wise. Should a person earn the trust of others or, do you verify the facts from reliable sources? What truths of God have you rejected as false because society embraces an opposing position?

Before receiving anything as accurate, even your thoughts, verify it according to God's Word to determine the truth. Truth, whole truth, never changes. Much of society no longer believes in absolute truths as they prefer to trust their feelings as the truth, but emotions are subject to change. You can trust the Bible to reveal how to live because it is the infallible Word of God. God is entirely trustworthy. Ask God for his discernment and wisdom.

Reflect

What worldly beliefs have you accepted as Truth when they are contrary to God's Word?

Scriptures

Psalms 19:7–8, 12
Psalms 32:6–7
Philippians 1:9–11
Hebrews 4:12

24

Kathi's Influence

Walk with the wise and become wise, for
a companion of fools suffers harm.
—Proverbs 13:20 (NIV)

Devotional

Kathi's friendship was a godly influence on my life. We shared many of the same interests, including our love for our Creator.

This one specific day was of beginnings and endings, highs and lows of life. Life is ever-changing, and at the same time, "there is nothing new under the sun." We talked about her diagnosis, treatment plan, and feelings during my visit. She was hopeful and looking forward to being healed but preferred not to focus on herself.

She wanted to hear about my summer vacation. We bent over my cell phone and shared photos of what inspired me. The images, plus her urging, caused me to read several heavenly insights, which inspired each photograph. A sense of excitement and energy was in the air because I had never shared my writings with anyone else. She encouraged me to write and became the instrument God used to ignite and fulfill his divine purpose for my life. All hesitation and uncertainty lifted from me. Her reassurance gave me the courage to write about the seemingly insignificant things in an ordinary day, which suddenly sparks my awareness of our heavenly Father and births another nugget of his truth into my spirit. He is evident everywhere. Search for him, and he will reveal himself.

The precious memory is so bittersweet, both glorious and heartbreaking. It was our last time together. Kathi never had any idea how her words had affected me. Her words were a turning point in more than one way. Little did I know while I was taking my first step toward God's vision by sharing divine revelations, he was also closing a door. My friend would not live to share my triumphs and joy. She will not be here to hold my hand through this process of trusting God in the unknown.

But I, like Kathi, am hopeful because of God's presence and promises.

Reflect

What vision has God placed in your heart to pursue? Have you received words of encouragement or defeat when you shared them?

Scriptures

Titus 2:7
Luke 6:40

25

No Sign of Life

When he was at the table with them, he took bread, gave thanks, broke it and began to give it to them. Then their eyes were opened and they recognized him, and he disappeared from their sight.
—Luke 24: 30–31 (NIV)

Devotional

Our next-door neighbor decides to have a small Fourth of July party, although the government limits people gathering. We are the only guests at their family cookout. It has become the norm for people to submit to having their temperature taken this year because anything above the standard 98.6 degrees indicates an infection. If above the normal range, the individual cannot enter and must quarantine.

Our friend has a new touchless thermometer to detect whether or not someone has a fever. The novelty of the latest gadget is entertaining. It is a rather solemn atmosphere until someone attempts to take my husband's temperature, then the celebration becomes comical because the device does not register anything. There is much fun-loving laughter as everyone tries to get the gadget to show his body's warmth. Regardless of the different angles and distances, the display screen remains blank. He is alive, so obviously, his body is generating heat. Eventually, we decided it is impossible to get results from the thermometer regarding his body. It is such a strange situation, so I ponder why it did not respond to him since his body remains warm to the touch. I think of a cold body as lifeless.

While thinking about people lacking signs of life, I wonder if there are people in our midst who are genuinely void of life. I do not mean they are dead, but they only exist and do not see what is around them. Blindness can be either physical or spiritual. The spark that causes a person to live their lives to the fullest is not there. Their lives are void and without purpose or vision. God has several warnings about not perceiving things in the spiritual realm. God wants us to walk with spiritual eyes wide open in wonder, beholding the majesty and goodness of God, which is the reason for the hope of eternal life.

In Acts, we learn that Saul has eyesight but is spiritually visionless until the light from heaven strikes him. Suddenly he becomes blind, physically unable to see, but receives spiritual sight and immediately recognizes and is obedient to instructions from God. He is no longer without vision spiritually, even though his ability to see naturally doesn't return until a short time later.

Reflect

Do you believe a person can observe Christian principles and be spiritually dead? How would you define it?

Scriptures

Acts 9:1–6
2 Corinthians 4:18

26

Persevere

He gives strength to the weary and increases the power of the weak. Even youths grow tired and weary, and young men stumble and fall; but those who hope in the Lord will renew their strength. They will soar on wings like eagles; they will run and not grow weary, they will walk and not be faint.

—Isaiah 40:29–31 (NIV)

Devotional

Do your everyday activities require you to develop certain regular habits? During my career, a healthy pattern was to retire for the evening and wake up at specific times because of work-related necessity. The same daily schedule was a disciplined part of my life for several years. I recently experienced an inability to fall asleep after going to bed in the evening but continued to rise at the usual time. Since I wasn't getting adequate rest, my energy level declined drastically, yet I told myself that self-control was a desirable quality.

Even when exhausted, I groggily yawned, stretched, and forced myself to get up at the sound of the alarm. Whenever the loud annoying buzzer went off, it compelled me to rise. One day I resolved to stay beneath the soft covers until my body felt restored. So I lingered quietly upon the plush mattress after waking up and eventually drifted off into slumber. Hours later, I awakened energized and leaped from the bed.

I deliberated about my understanding of the meaning of the word *persevere*. I viewed the action of getting out of bed and remaining steadfast in daily practice as diligence in pressing on toward a goal. It was adamantly moving forward with my efforts. However, my recent ability to obtain sleep through continuing to remain in a restful state caused me to reach a different conclusion. To endure is more than an act of moving on. It may be remaining still in a state of rest or reflection. Endurance is essential in our spiritual life. We don't always have to be working or studying. Rather than being determined to advance toward a goal, sometimes we benefit more by humbly remaining in his presence, keeping a state of meditation with God. There is much to consider about abiding in him.

Reflect

Think about a time when you persevered in your walk with Christ. Were there times of pressing on with stamina as well as times of stillness as you press into God's presence for his power to remain faithful? Which brought you closer to the Lord?

Scriptures

James 1:2–4
John 15:5
Romans 5:1–4

27

Snake Bite

May the God of hope fill you with all joy
and peace as you trust in him, so that you
may overflow with hope by the power of
the Holy Spirit.

—Romans 15:13 (NIV)

Devotional

The desolate two-lane highway weaved through the forest
from one side of the remote area to the other side. There were
canals on both sides with very few homes along its route. Off
the country road in the middle of acres of fields stood the
stately two-story farmhouse reminiscent of olden days. The
wooden structure had weathered years as a shelter for families
who enjoyed a carefree life in the country miles away from
town.

We saw several deer grazing upon tall golden grass on
the opposite side of the large pond. The herd was a reasonable

distance from the house, in a serene natural setting. Quietly, we crept closer for a better view of the graceful bodies of the white-tailed doe with her fawn. Our young daughter was a step behind her dad as he separated the tall blades of grass with his arms to make way for her to tiptoe behind him quietly. Lagging behind her, I carried the youngest child on my hip. Living in the country afforded us the peace we desired until sudden screams caught us by surprise. My child's cries that a snake had bitten her filled me with dread. Our home was in a remote area of the county in a community with few houses and no medical facility.

The dispatcher for emergency calls instructed us to drive toward the emergency medical team, racing toward us. We decided we should meet them halfway between town and our home. My husband drove the car; my job was to reassure our daughter. She needed to stay calm so the venom would pump through her small body slowly. I was overwhelmed by uncontrollable panic. I couldn't give her peace and assurance that everything was fine since I was without peace. When the vehicles met, we hastily transferred our daughter to the ambulance, but the paramedic denied my entrance because I lacked the confidence and tranquility to comfort her. The marks indicated that of a poisonous snake. Snakes are not aggressive and may not release venom if discouraged by clothing or shoes. Although the snake's fangs penetrated her shoe and left puncture marks on her ankle, the shoe protected her from harm to some degree, so she did not receive full venom. She was given an anti-venomous vaccination and had to keep her leg elevated for several days. The scar is still visible today.

Sadly, God will deny people entrance into heaven because they lack the necessary faith and confidence in Jesus Christ. Our loving God made a way to justify us by the atonement of sins through the death and resurrection of his only Son. There is no other way to be redeemed from the curse of sin.

Reflect

Was there a time when you lacked the peace of God? What caused you to lose harmony with God, and how could you have maintained his peace?

Scriptures

John 3:16
Acts 10:36
2 Thessalonians 3:16

28

Soul Where Are You?

"Very truly I tell you, whoever hears my
word and believes him who sent me has
eternal life and will not be judged but has
crossed over from death to life."
                              —John 5:24 (NIV)

Devotional

The loss of a person who is significant in your life is a crush-
ing experience. At first, there is denial. Then suffering and a
wish to see, reach out, and touch this person who brought
meaning to life. The idea that viewing the body will confirm
it is only a bad dream isn't realistic, but the desire to believe
the individual is still alive is strong. Death seems so final.
Filled with unbelief and bewilderment, you hesitantly step
closer to where the body lay to stare at the still form. Casting
eyes upon the lifeless body, at once, it is evident the living
soul has vanished. What is left is death and a dim reminder

of the absence of the love of your life. Gone are the gentle glow upon the skin and the sparkle of joy in the eyes. All the qualities that were such a part of the individual have vanished. Even the loving touch of the hand meets with cold and indifference rather than warmth and welcoming.

The dead body that lay there is not the person but the remains left behind when he departed. The moment somehow reassures you. The soul is alive in another place. In essence, the soul of the person has left the body. The body is a mere shell that once housed the soul. It brings a reality the soul has exited the body and is residing elsewhere.

God breathed into Adam the breath of life. He instantly became a living person. Although a person's soul is invisible, we see evidence of the living soul in every individual. Proof of God is all around us as well. His creation is evidence of his existence as the intricacies are impossible and must be the hand of God's supremacy. Search for proof of God in scripture and throughout our world full of his marvelous works.

Reflect

What evidence in your life validates faith in God?

Scriptures

Romans 1:20
Genesis 2:7
John 1:2–4
John 5:28–30

29

Storm Driven Rain

But blessed are your eyes because they
see, and your ears because they hear. For
truly I tell you, many prophets and righteous people longed to see what you see
but did not see it, and to hear what you
hear but did not hear it.
—Matthew 13:16–17 (NIV)

Devotional

Driving through the outer fringes of a tropical storm is
frightening. The eyes of the operator must not drift off the
road for a second. There is an immediate danger because of
the pounding rain limiting vision. Everything is a blur. A
glance from the roadway or a scan of the eyes may result in
missing a hazardous road condition, such as the potholes or
vehicles ahead. The windshield of the car has a continuous
spray of torrential rain; everything else fades into obscurity.

The onslaught of water washes away the view. A person must focus intently on the road to recognize objects and correctly perceive distances because it is crucial. An alert driver looks intently, focusing both eyes and mind. This person wants to remain aware of obstructions or hazards in the path, to pass safely through the storm.

Just as the driver focuses on the road, our primary focus is Christ and making every effort to live according to God's will. Learning isn't casual reading; it involves comprehension, acting upon what the Holy Spirit reveals, and self-examination. Intently observing innermost thoughts and motives is imperative; therefore, do everything possible to grow godly attributes such as goodness, knowledge, and self-control.

When lacking insight, examine God's Word, searching for divine knowledge. Ask for the understanding to uncover his truth rightly because how we perceive concerns may not be correct, but our perception determines our actions. God warns about seeing but not spiritually comprehending what he is doing in the world. A real awareness of the spiritual realm is discernment from the Lord.

Reflect

Do you believe it is possible to see something with your natural eyes but not perceive the spiritual forces at work in the situation, whether God or demonic? Then ask God to reveal the concealed truth.

Scriptures

1 Corinthians 2:14–16
Isaiah 43:18–19
Luke 9:45
2 Peter 1:5–8

30

Surrender Our Fears

> Do not conform to the pattern of this world, but be transformed by the renewing of your mind. Then you will be able to test and approve what God's will is-his good, pleasing and perfect will.
>
> —Romans 12:2 (NIV)

Devotional

God calls all to a life of devotion and yielding our will to his good and acceptable will. God wants everyone to love him passionately.

Do we hold back a little piece of ourselves from God because we are selfish or insecure? The feeling of control is false security. Sometimes we do not commune with God or study his Word thoroughly. Lack of knowledge creates doubt. If we allow fear to overpower us, we are more likely to be disobedient; instead of kneeling to God in prayer, we bow to our fears and doubts in defeat rather than risking our lives for our incredible Savior?

God's Word transforms. By standing for godly principles, we are set apart from others and do not conform to the world's standards. Fear of being isolated or persecuted is not from God. Jesus came into this world to bring peace, atonement for sin, and not confusion or fear.

People are often self-centered and wish to remain where they feel comfortable. Jesus sacrificed his life for all, and in gratitude and thanks, we, in return, submit to him daily. There is nothing easy about surrender. It takes stepping out in faith and having courage even when afraid. We walk in obedience, total devotion, and dependence on God and his mighty power in times of weakness because he is ready and able to meet every need and free us of fear. Numerous times, the Bible instructs us not to fear.

Reflect

What fears or insecurities do you wrestle with, and how do you overcome those feelings?

Scripture

Psalms 51:12
Jeremiah 29:11
Joshua 1:9
John 16:33

31

Remove the Masks

But whenever anyone turns to the Lord,
the veil is taken away. Now the Lord is
the Spirit, and where the Spirit of the
Lord is, there is freedom. And we all,
who with unveiled faces contemplate
the Lord's glory, are being transformed
into his image with ever-increasing glory,
which comes from the Lord, who is the
Spirit.
  —2 Corinthians 3:16–18 (NIV)

Devotional

Masks are not only a piece of cloth covering our faces; when
we hide our true identity, we cover the truth. Undetectable
veils are harder to perceive because they are invisible. They
do not hide physical traits; they conceal wrong thoughts,
emotions, motives, and agendas. People cover up insecurities

and even evil, which deceives the innocent. We are all guilty of concealing our flaws when we should ask God to help us overcome them. Remember, Satan aims to destroy us, so be aware of his schemes.

God is ushering in a time of awakening. It is time to remove self-doubt that covers our mouths and prevents us from sharing, *spreading* the Gospel of Christ, and proclaiming the good news of redemption. He calls us to share his forgiveness and his love for us with others. It is such a simple concept yet challenging to exemplify because we often crave acceptance and honor from others more than we desire God's presence.

We say we love him, yet out of fear of rejection, we fail to share that love story. Instead, we choose omission, which is denial. We sometimes forget our lives, and words are to reflect on him. Is he the desire of our lives? Are our thoughts and conversations about his love for us? Each of us may be the only likeness of Jesus others see. We cannot allow the world to silence our praise and worship of him. Let us remove our masks so others can see Christ in us.

Reflect

Imagine the result of turning to God and releasing all burdens and weaknesses to him. What does it feel like to be free of masks that hide your true identity?

Scriptures

Romans 12:2
Proverbs 26:24

Prayer of Salvation

Dear Lord, I love you and want to live my life for you. I have sinned, I repent, and I ask for your forgiveness. I have confidence you are the Son of God, crucified and rose from the dead, that I may have forgiveness and eternal life. Amen

Romans 3:23
Romans 6:1–2
Romans 6:23
Romans 10:9–10
Romans 10:13
Ephesians 2:8–9
1 John 1:9